## About the Author

Alicia Gough is thirty-five years old and lives with her parents near Chester. She was born with a physical disability, cerebral palsy. Her supportive family have always encouraged her to lead a full and active life. With charm, a sense of humour and a sunny friendliness, Alicia has always fought against the stereotyping of disability, determined from an early age to be listened to, to achieve educational and physical challenges, to show emphatically that those with a disability can enjoy interesting, purposeful lives. She has always expressed her feelings, thoughts and ideas through her poetry and stories and writing.

# Dedication

This book is dedicated to the memory of my brother Stuart.

Alicia Gough

# THE HAND THAT TELLS THE STORY: LIVING WITH MY DISABILITY

AUSTIN MACAULEY PUBLISHERS™

LONDON · CAMBRIDGE · NEW YORK · SHARJAH

A CIP catalogue record for this title is available from the British Library.

ISBN 9781528988438 (Paperback)
ISBN 9781528988445 (ePub e-book)

www.austinmacauley.com

First Published (2021)
Austin Macauley Publishers Ltd
25 Canada Square
Canary Wharf
London
E14 5LQ

# Acknowledgements

Meeting my old teacher from Dorin Park School, Pauline Sallis mid-way through 2017 gave me the inspiration to fulfil an ambition to write a book.

Pauline's help and guidance to this effect, has been amazing and I will be forever grateful.

I must also thank Katie Buckley, my valued support worker, who has worked tirelessly putting pen to paper.

Many thanks to Liz Roberts for all her kindness and help and support.

Mum and Dads support, as always has been great. Gentle reminders regarding my early years have been invaluable.

# Table of Contents

# Synopsis

My book is a memoir, showing how I have lived with my disability. It describes my early years and my reactions to realising that I was disabled and could not talk or walk. I describe my school days, how important my friends were, what I enjoyed and didn't enjoy.

I have a chapter showing the importance of finding the best ways to communicate, and how having my present communicator has made such a wonderful difference to my life. I ask to be given time and patience to communicate, to be treated with respect and to be listened to.

A chapter shows how having a job that I was good at gave me such joy and a sense of purpose and how devastated I was when it ended.

My family have been very important to me. I describe our happiness and sadness, and all the great people in it.

I have a chapter about all our wonderful travels, the amazing places we've visited.

I conclude my memoir by celebrating all my achievements and the exciting experiences which have enriched my life.

The book hopefully shows that I have achieved a lot in my thirty-five years, that my life has been positive, exciting and eventful. Life can be fun!

I have also included a selection of relevant photographs and poems that I have written over the years.

# Introduction

I'm Ave from Argentina. I would like to tell you, you are an INSPIRATION for all of us, so CONGRATULATIONS! I think you're so lucky with your awesome family and friends and that is something to be grateful for, isn't it? I'm very happy to read your story. DON'T STOP! NEVER! You are amazing!
– Ave

I loved it, every word. I'm going to pass it on to my sister who is scared of disability. Hopefully, the book will give her more understanding. Everyone should read it.
– Jean Dyson

The things you have done in your life make me think anything in life is possible.
– Peter and Chris

Keep writing. We want to hear more of your adventures.
– Jill and John

I'm over the moon for you. It is wonderful that your creativity is being taken seriously.
– Di Brown

Alicia, you are an inspiration to us all. Life is as much fun as we make it and you make buckets of fun!
– Mauve

How moved we were reading your book. It made us cry.
– Jill and Kevin

Don't forget me when you're famous. You are amazing!
– Shelley

Wow! How powerful the words from someone who cannot speak. To have such an insight into the world is humbling.
– Sylv

I'm sure your book will travel and give happiness to everyone who reads it.
– Glen Cooper

### Ad Librum Suum

My little book who will thou please, tell me,
All which shall read thee? No, that cannot be.
Whom then, the best? But few of these are known.
How shalt thou know to please, thou know'st not whom?
The meaner sort commend not poetry:
And sure the worst should please themselves for thee:
But let them pass, and set by most no store,
Please thou one well, thou shall not need please more.
– Thomas Bastard (1566–1618)

# Chapter One
## How Do I Belong in the World?

Hi! My name is Alicia. I was a big surprise to my Mum and Dad when I was born as my brothers were eleven and fifteen years old. I was born extra special to all my family.

I'm really excited to be writing this story.

I would like to let you know what it's like to be disabled. It's not just about being in a wheelchair.

It's about finding where and how I belong in the world.

What is my disability? I was born with cerebral palsy. Cerebral palsy is caused through a lack of oxygen to the brain usually at the time of birth. It affects the muscles in the body. Everyone with cerebral palsy is different. I am athetoid. Athetoid cerebral palsy is damage to the brain affecting muscle control and speech.

I went to a special school when I was three as I couldn't walk and couldn't talk, at least not verbally. I've always got lots to say and I make sure everyone knows what I'm trying to say. My family and friends say I never shut up.

My carer Katie said,

"I was very worried that I would be unable to understand or know what you needed when your parents were not around but after two shifts, I just understood you even without words." She knows everything I want or need now and can't believe she was ever worried.

She thinks I'm amazing at communicating.

So, I'm a good communicator even if it takes some time for people to understand.

I want to tell my own story so that everyone can understand about disabilities.

When I look back to my childhood, I remember how there was always family and friends around at the house; me, Mum, Dad, my brothers Stuart and Simon, Nan Bet, Auntie Pat, Marlon my nephew, and the dog, Blod. Simon and Stuart, my brothers, would greet me every morning with "Good morning" and pull my ponytail.

My brothers were full of fun and I loved them and still love them very much. I wrote this poem to them.

## My Brothers

My brothers are always joking with me.
They make me laugh.
They let me hear their music.
I like it loud.
They phone me once a month.
They tell me their news.
They send postcards when on holiday
In Tunisia.
My brothers, they love me.

Simon wrote this about me.

## My Sister Alicia

I was fifteen, almost sixteen, when Alicia was born and at first, we had no idea she was different from any other baby. When we did find out, it didn't make any difference to me because she was my sister.

My brother Stuart and I helped out as much as we could with looking after Alicia. We would feed her breakfast but would flick Rice Krispies at her. Most of them would end up all over her face! Alicia would laugh her head off! And we made sure she was always laughing and we still do by saying rude things or telling rude jokes. When she was about two years old, we taught her how to stick her two fingers up at the Breakfast TV weather girl Wincey Willis because she was so annoying every morning telling the weather. Then whenever we asked Alicia to 'do a Wincey' she would stick her fingers up at people!

My Mum went to keep fit every Wednesday and we looked after Alicia. Almost every week she would have a dirty nappy that needed changing and we hated having to change them! Alicia would do everything she could to NOT help us trying to change it!

When Alicia was older and got her first electric chair, we would set up assault courses to help her train for her school sports day. She loved it especially when we rigged the speed setting on her wheelchair and she would zoom around really fast! But if she went around the course the wrong way or crashed or something, she would go mad and try to run over Stuart and me!

When I left home when Alicia was seven years old she loved all the rough and tumble on the living room carpet but since then she has gone through being a young lady, a troublesome, fashion-conscious 'girl power' teenager into an intelligent and popular young lady with expensive tastes in clothes, so much so my wife is forever asking to borrow her clothes when we go to visit! But no matter what, she's my little sister who will always laugh at my jokes, especially the dirty ones!

I certainly remember Mum sometimes asking one of them to feed me and they would mess about flicking food around. Another of their jokes was that they'd pretend Nana had come to visit us pretending my Nan was knocking at the front door and I would get all excited!

Just thinking about my Nan again makes me happy.

I can still hear her call to Mum, "Put on that kettle and make it snappy!"

Nan Bet was very kind.

I loved my Nana Bet very much. She would play with me and take me out. She seemed to think I liked walking around the cemetery! I liked it better when she pushed me on the swing in the local park.

Here's a photo of Nan playing with me on the floor in my bedroom. You can see how tightly I've got my arms around her neck. I nearly pulled her over. She read to me lovely fairy stories and always bought me books for Christmas. When she was reading, she'd leave out words and then I'd have to find them, like she'd read 'the big bad...' and I'd have to point at 'wolf'. That way she helped to teach me to read. Our favourite book to read together was *Heidi*.

Here's a poem I wrote about her:

**My Nan**
My Nan was very kind.
Another like her is hard to find.
She had lovely white hair, and a heart full of loving care.
On a beautiful day with sunny blue skies
Was like looking out of my nan's bright blue eyes.
In my bedroom, Nan and I played for hours
Pretending that we had magical powers.
My Nan was really quite small.
She made me feel six foot tall.
When I think of my Nan it makes me happy.
I can still hear her call to Mum,
"Put on that kettle and make it snappy!"

Grampy, my Granddad, was very thoughtful but he was always telling jokes. He was always singing to me. He had a lovely voice. He sang *The Grand Old Duke of York* so often that Mum asked him if he knew any other songs. He told funny stories too. One of my favourite stories that he told was about what happened when the fair came to Chester in May, the same time as the races which Grampy also loved. He liked to have a bet on the horses. At the fair, a ring was set up. There was a professional boxer, a really big bloke. The ringmaster would say to the crowd,

"Is there anyone who dares to challenge him?"

My Grampy put his hand up every time. He always won and then he'd collect all the money that had been thrown into the ring. Well, one time the ringmaster said to Grampy after he'd knocked out the professional boxer, "You're a professional boxer. You're not taking that money!"

All the crowd starting booing and the ringmaster had to give Grampy the money. Grampy probably used the money he'd won to have a bet at the races. Mum always remembers him coming home and Nan saying, "How much have you won?"

"Not much," he'd say.

Then he'd get all his winnings out of his pocket and share it with all the family. He was always very generous. When he came to see me, he'd put his hands in his pockets, take out some money and say, "Go and buy yourself something nice."

Grampy was also a wonderful cook. Mum remembers the chocolate cake he made for my birthday, really tall and covered in chocolate buttons. He made the best pancakes and could toss the pancakes really high. Once he threw a pancake so high it stuck on the ceiling!

Recently I was looking through a book and I found a poem I'd written about Grampy when I was about thirteen. Here it is.

**My Gramps**

My Gramps is full of fun.
He knows how to make me laugh
When I feel glum.
He bakes the best ever cakes
And juggles with eggs till one breaks!
He tells me about the olden days.
Everyone was called Whatshisname.
It could be just a phase,
Making homemade is one of his hobbies.
He tells us it's good for pain that niggles
But it always gives my Mum giggles.
He loves a bet on the horses.
He often has a win.
Now I know why I also
Have this habit under my skin.
In Spring, he spends his days planting seeds.
One year when they popped out of the soil
They just looked like weeds!
I love my Gramps.
He makes me feel happy.
He tells me jokes.
Some old, some new.
Without my Gramps
What would I do!

It was my Grampy who helped me learn the alphabet by numbers. He would test me every time he came to see me so that I could communicate better. My hand told the story. Then to make it easy for people to understand me, we put the alphabet onto an A4 sheet in numerical order. I realised people didn't recognise the alphabet by numbers. It doesn't take long though for most people to catch on. Some people were quick on the alphabet. Some people found it difficult. Mum said to people, "Write down the letters as they come to help you to remember."

I got very quick. Mum was the best. My sister Karen was good too. Even though I've now got my eye gaze, I still use the alphabet method to communicate – the hand that tells the story – this is how the book got its name.

I always remember Auntie Pat coming around and doing my exercises with me. I think it was always an excuse to come around for a brew and natter with my Mum.

My Mum told me I was born in Chester weighing eight pounds seven ounces. I was a big baby. Dad was working away in Saudi Arabia and didn't get to meet me until I was seven weeks old. I had to stay in the hospital for two weeks because I was very poorly.

I had to have physio every week. The physiotherapist used to come to our house. I also had a standing frame that I was strapped to for an hour or so. Mum said she wanted to get me a baby walker but was told no.

My Grampy used to hold me and let me try walk. I loved it but the physio told Grampy that it was not good for me, but did he stop? NO!

As I got older and stronger with Mum's help I learnt to crawl which was quite a surprise to the physio and paediatrician. I also went swimming with Mum in a special warm pool from three months old. The pool was at the school I eventually went to.

When I was about six years old, I was playing in my bedroom with Gina, my cousin, who is five years older than me. I played a lot with Gina. We're still close. She's part of my family. My Mum tells me she was a bridesmaid at my Mum and Dad's wedding. She's married now with two children of her own.

Our favourite game was hairdressers. I had long hair and Gina loved to brush and comb it, sometimes a bit too hard.

"More gently Gina," her Mum, Aunty Angela, would say. We played school and Gina was always the teacher. I had a lovely white and pink tea set and she would make us cups of tea. Imagine then one day I noticed I was different when Gina asked me why I was in a wheelchair and nobody else was. I didn't realise before as I wasn't treated any differently to the other children in my family. Gina also asked why I couldn't talk.

I had been so happy with my family. I never realised I was different and had a disability. I felt mixed up, and not understanding at the time what it all meant. Why was I in a wheelchair? Why couldn't I talk? Was I going to be like this for forever? I had no idea what it all meant. I used to play on the floor at home and crawl from room to room. When I went out in my wheelchair, I felt different. I never felt upset really. I was more frustrated.

If you were me which would you choose, to be able to walk or talk? I remember thinking I would choose to talk because the wheelchair speaks for itself. It's hard this one, a difficult choice, but I suppose what I want to say is that I wanted people to hear my voice.

Another thing I remember is Scope coming to film me at home for the video to be sent to other centres across the country. They just wanted to see how I was progressing after I was diagnosed with cerebral palsy. They gave me a toy monkey. He was so cuddly. I have still got him. I call him Joey.

I think they had chosen me because I was not shy and was used to having my photo taken. I always smiled, Mum said, when a camera was around.

Mealtimes were always a problem. I so wished I could have my meals without assistance. I remember wanting a pottery plate and not a plastic one. I was quite young. My Mum says I was only two or three. And at school, I wanted to feed myself. There was a thing called a Neater-Eater which was to help control your hand movement. It did help with the tremor but then it was trying to get the food off the spoon. It made my head shake instead! Very funny. It did help with my hands but couldn't do anything about the movement of my head.

I was so disappointed because independence was so important to me. I was always up for trying something new! In the nursery, I always wanted to sit in a chair like most of the other children, not in my first tiny power chair. I was always very independent. I wanted to be independent. I didn't like everything being done for me.

I'm really excited to be writing this story. I would like to let you know what it's like to be disabled. It's not just about being in a wheelchair. It's about finding where and how I belong in the world.

# Chapter Two
## With a Little Help from My Friends: Schooldays

I didn't think my school was different at the time. I was only about three. I knew I was going to a different school when the family talked about the school. They would say the school needed to help me more. I understood a little bit what they meant. At the time I didn't think I did need help. I thought I was OK. I'm glad though that they did talk to me because it helped me to understand the situation. The best thing about school was having friends the same as me. I am not alone. Yes, it made me feel happy in big ways. We can help each other.

We all learnt the alphabet together. That helped us. The ones, like me, who couldn't talk would point to the letters. Only three of us in the class could talk. They would say the letters.

One of our lovely assistants, Debbie, would help us to play and get on together. She would put us in groups to play games together. I remember she always helped me to hold a very fat thick crayon so I could draw pictures.

One of my very best friends was Donna. She wore splints and she could walk around. If I pointed to any toy or game Donna would get them for me. She left our school when she was eight and I remember how sad I felt.

Another of my friends was Richard. He liked pushing me around in my chair. Richard was very funny. He was always making me laugh. One of his tricks was taking the pictures down from the wall and hiding them.

One Christmas, Richard and I were Mary and Joseph in the nativity play. One of the girls tried to take the baby Jesus out of my arms. Richard pushed her away.

My Mum and Kurt's Mum used to love Nativity plays. While all the other mums would be crying with sadness, my Mum and Kurt's Mum would be crying with laughter! My Mum loves to tell me the story of when Kurt was playing the part of one of the kings. My Mum noticed he wasn't secured properly in his wheelchair. As he was coming up to give his gift to the baby Jesus, Kurt started to tip out of his chair. His golden crown fell off and rolled all over the hall. Luckily Kurt didn't fall out, and he was secured properly and had his crown put back on!

My very best friend was and still is Kurt. Kurt is funny. He talks to me and we get the giggles together.
He says, "I understand you Alicia."

I went to stay at his house every week for ten years.

We did have our ups and downs though. Every sports day Kurt won the wheelchair race, year in, year out, but then one year, FINALLY, I won! Kurt was so annoyed that I had finally beat him after all those years of him winning. We also captured my victory with the camera!

Another time I wanted to play football with the boys on the playground but the girls had to sit at the side and just watch. We were not allowed to play, but I wasn't having any of it! So I asked Mum if it would be OK for me to play, and she said why not and to ask the boys if they didn't mind – the answer was yes, I could play, and I scored a goal first time! I loved it.

My Mum and Dad looked into my going to mainstream school but realised that I would have missed out on the swimming pool, occupational therapist, speech therapist and physio, all of them based in Dorin Park School. We had a family meeting and decided against the mainstream school. I think if I'd have gone to mainstream school I wouldn't have liked the fuss about my disability. I also might have been placed in a unit for those children who had learning problems, had problems learning to read and write. I would really have hated that.

I can imagine that some of the kids would have been messing about with my wheelchair, especially as mine was an electric wheelchair.

Getting around the school in a wheelchair would have been difficult anyway. Although it's not that long ago mainstream schools were not equipped to cope with a disability like mine.

When I was about ten, I had a short break from my English school when Dad went to work in Dubai. I went to a special school while we were there. I went from eight in the morning till one o'clock as it was very hot. I would then come back home in the afternoon and have sleep. I was the only pupil from Britain.

I do still remember my teacher's name was Merium. She was an Indian lady. The headteacher was an Egyptian lady, the physio was from Sweden, and the speech therapist was English. In the school at Dubai, there were lots of books for me to work in. I had no problem in understanding them. The work was good. It made you think. There were also good books for me to read.

There was a range of disability. It was a small school about thirty to forty pupils. It was good having teachers of all nationalities. It made the school very interesting. It sort of gave you a good understanding of the world.

It was a great adventure.

We were in Dubai for six months.

I celebrated my tenth birthday there. Mum and Dad bought me a watch.

I remember so many things. I remember we had to go shopping in the evening at about seven o'clock when it was much cooler. The shopping malls were amazing, the biggest I have seen in my life. When Dad came home from work, we would go swimming. We went every day. Dad belonged to a club for expatriates so we would swim there at his club and not on the beach. If you swam on the beach you would have to be fully clothed. You couldn't have swimwear on.

The Arab people were very nice and friendly. They would often give me a small gift when we visited the souks. The souks are like our markets but on a much more massive scale. Everything seemed to be huge. There was a special souk which only sold gold. I have never seen so many stalls selling just gold.

One of my favourite things was having a trip across the creek in a dhow which is a ferry boat. The ferrymen would just lift me and my wheelchair on to the boat with no effort at all.

One time we travelled across the desert in a jeep with Dad's friends to a beach resort called Korfakhan. On the way, we passed herds of camels. There were camel rides on the beach. I was asked did I fancy a ride but I said no thanks!

I remember there was a sandstorm. Dad picked me up out of my chair. Some teenagers were going past and one of them took off his cap and gave it to me to put on my head.

I was sorry in some ways when I left the school but glad too. I was ready to go home. One thing I really missed was not being able to go outside because it was so very hot.

Dad phoned the headmaster to see if I could return to my old school.

"Of course, Mr Gough. We'll be very pleased to see her."

So I went back on a Monday morning in September. I remember it was Project Week. All my friends cheered when they saw me. Kurt had cried all the way home when he knew

28

I was going to Dubai! I was so pleased to see everyone again, all my friends. At first though, when I returned to Dorin Park I didn't know what was going on. I felt confused. One of the carers though took time to help me catch up with my work. It took me three weeks to catch up.

I was glad to get home. Home's best!

When I was about fourteen though I did want to go to another school because I found the work too easy. I worked more quickly than the rest of the class. I would have to wait for them to finish. I would be fed up and angry. Why don't the teachers give me more work? Sometimes I got so fed up I would drive out of the classroom. I got into trouble all of the time but I didn't care.

I loved the swimming pool. I felt freedom. The warm water helped with my body. It made it feel relaxed. I would have liked to have gone swimming every day, even if only for fifteen minutes.

I would also have liked to have worked towards qualifications. I would have liked to have known what I could achieve. I found it all very frustrating. It would have been good to have got a certificate at the end of each term.

It was good when young people came into the school to work with us.

I remember we had a lovely group of young people who did artwork with us. They bought new fresh ideas. Having young people around the school was exciting. We loved them coming into the playground with us, playing games and talking to us. Talking with us was the best.

Drama made me feel excited. At the end of the lesson, we always wanted to know what we'd be doing next week. Everybody did. We all put the play together. I remember I was Aunt Emily in *The Wizard of Oz*. Over the years at Dorin Park, there were lots of different plays. We did them at the end of each term, different kinds of plays for Easter, Christmas and so on. And we marked national and world events too. I remember two plays especially, *JC2000* and *A Midsummer Night's Dream*. I really liked *A Midsummer Night's Dream*.

The play *JC2000* marked the millennium 2000. Forty of us on two coaches to go to the Bridgewater Hall in Manchester. Imagine. I remember it was the year 2000 in the month of March on a Tuesday evening. It was really exciting. It was the first time the school had ever done anything like this, this really big event. We had started practising the play before Christmas. Chris was the narrator and he spoke some words at the beginning of the play. The words were about not worrying about your life. He said:

Look at the lilies of the field. They reap not, neither do they sow. Look at the birds of the air. They neither sow nor reap. Therefore do not worry about tomorrow. Tomorrow will take care of itself.

I also remember three of us, me, Celyn and Debbie did a dance at Chester University. It was the first public performance outside the school that I had taken part in. We had beautiful material to float around and we all went around in a circle in our wheelchairs. I also remember that we had to keep quiet about it because there was only us three in the dance and we knew that others might be a bit upset.

I said to Mrs Brown, "How are we going to work this one out? We won't have time to practise."

We sorted it out by practising in the lunch hour!

I always felt sad when someone like a student who'd been helping us left. It was good having their new ideas.

When I was seventeen, I was happy to move on, to do new things.

Looking back on my school days what would I say to the staff?

Listen more. And get more young people in the school and ask for their advice.

# Chapter Three
## Let Your Eyes Talk

My Mum asked me the question, "Would you prefer to walk or talk?"

I said I would choose to talk. I wished the school had asked me that question. They seemed to want me to walk more than to talk. Why didn't the school ask me this question?

I often wondered why the school never asked me about myself or the situation I was in.

Why didn't the school ask me this question?

Why didn't they try to understand what my voice was telling them?

Why did they give me so very little time with the speech therapist? Why not every day not just once a week? Speech therapy helped my breathing. Breathing in a controlled slow way helped me to relax. When I'm relaxed I'm able to say single words like 'mum' and 'Ian'. My Mum says my favourite word to say when I was little was 'more' because I loved my food so much!

When I can come out with single words, I feel excited.

Relaxation is very important. If I put my hands between my knees my body becomes calm and involuntary movement is controlled. When I'm relaxed I can concentrate. I can express my ideas. It's important to get across what you are thinking and feeling. I've got lots of ideas I want to share. I didn't talk to those people in school who didn't understand my situation. It was hard to make friends with them. Some of the staff were best at understanding me and some didn't give me the time to listen. How important is it to listen to each other?

It's very important. Everyone's got opinions and feelings whether or not they have a disability.

When people don't take time to listen I feel frustrated and angry.

To help me walk I had a standing frame with wheels that I had to hold onto. My left hand couldn't grip it for long. And it took me so long to get anywhere. After a few weeks, one day, after I had been walking down the corridor on the standing frame, I got so angry I went back to class and communicated to the staff how upset I was. I expressed my feeling about it.

"It's taking me half an hour to get halfway down the corridor. I could have been in the classroom ages ago doing my work if I'd been using my electric wheelchair."

One of the teachers wrote down my objections and rang up my Mum.

Mum said, "Well you know Alicia. She's got a mind of her own."

Thankfully soon after this, the walking experiment with the standing frame ended.

My friend Kurt always said to me, "Concentrate on talking and writing."

Then the school finally advised us to get a communication aid. At last, when I was eight, the school got me a Liberator. Unfortunately, some of the staff couldn't use it and it would be locked away in a cupboard. The staff completely lacked understanding about it. I felt like I had to teach some of them to use it.

With the Liberator, you had to press down on the right symbol. Due to my involuntary movements, this was difficult and I was very limited in what I could say. I did have several other communication aids throughout the years, one being called DynaVox.

I found different ways of communicating. Everyone without the ability for verbal speech should have some form of a communication aid. I had a way of communicating by pointing to the letters from the alphabet and getting them typed by my carer. This is how I wrote my stories and poems.

One of my carers, Julie, was very helpful. I wrote this poem to her to thank her.

## Julie

I like Julie very much.
She laughs a lot.
She is kind to me.
She gives me my dinner
And talks to me all the time.
She has lovely blonde hair and shiny eyes.
I am glad
That Julie is my helper.

When I was in school, we took part in competitions to get our poems published in a book. When I was thirteen, I had my poem *My Dad* published in an anthology called *Future Voices*. Here's the poem I wrote about my Dad.

## My Dad

To describe my Dad,
I would start by saying
How special he is to me.
He has short black hair
Which my Mum would
like to be shorter.
I tease him about his
prickly face and
His old-fashioned clothes
Which try to hide his
stomach that wobbles.
His hobbies are betting on
the horses,

And supporting Manchester United – how sad.
How special is my Dad to me.

When I was fourteen, I had the poem about my brothers, *My Brothers*, published in an anthology called *Kaleidoscope*.

33

Writing poems has always been a very important part of my life. Sometimes I say to my Mum, "Mum, can you help me, I've got a poem in my head."

I like to write happy, new poems. Here's my happiness poem.

### Happiness

Happiness is how I feel.
Happiness sometimes doesn't seem real.
Happiness is a new-born child.
Happiness is to do something wild.
Happiness can make you cry.
Happiness makes the time fly.
Happiness is very nice.
Happiness should be kept on ice.
Happiness brings lots of luck.

Happiness is to read my favourite book.
Happiness is being with my friends.
Happiness is time that never ends.
Happiness has been writing my book.

And I like to write poems when I feel frustrated. I also write poems about new experiences. We did a project in school about Vietnam and that inspired me to write this poem. I wanted to show how a young person would feel because what young people feel could happen to anyone anywhere. The poem is about any young person.

**I am so sorry**

I am depressed upset and uncomfortable.
It is stormy in my head and I feel lost.
It is going bad.
I'm sorry for all the things I did.
I made so many mistakes with you.
My heart has stopped beating.
It was such a young age to die.
Every night I have nightmares
About the funeral.
I keep thinking about our holiday
And looking at the photos.
You loved me even though I forgot to tell you
Not to wear your jeans at the dance.
You were so kind and thoughtful.
I remember flirting,
Not realising how I was hurting you.
I am so sorry.

I had a close friend Chris. When I think of him, I remember he had a bit of a table on the front of his wheelchair, and I remember he played the part of the Scarecrow when we performed the play *The Wizard of Oz*. He became very ill and was taken into hospital. When I went to visit him in the hospital, I gave him the poem I had written for him. Here it is.

## Poem for Chris

As soon as we met
We became good friends,
Just one look and a smile
That never ends.
I think of you in the hospital.
I hope you're feeling better.
I thought you'd like this poem
Instead of a letter.
I hear you have

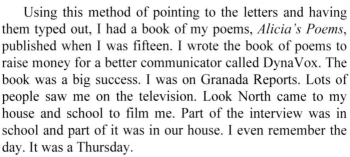

Tubes here and tubes everywhere.
Try not to worry.
The nurses will care.

Using this method of pointing to the letters and having them typed out, I had a book of my poems, *Alicia's Poems*, published when I was fifteen. I wrote the book of poems to raise money for a better communicator called DynaVox. The book was a big success. I was on Granada Reports. Lots of people saw me on the television. Look North came to my house and school to film me. Part of the interview was in school and part of it was in our house. I even remember the day. It was a Thursday.

My English teacher was interviewed too. I got some good feedback across the board.

My family and friends loved reading the poems about themselves and friends, and those in my family who didn't have a poem written about them would say to me,

"Why haven't you written a poem about me?"

We sold two hundred and fifty copies and so raised half of the money for my communicator. Mum and Dad and friends raised the other half with a sponsored walk up Snowdon.

My headteacher wrote about my book of poems in my National Record of Achievement:

Alicia started at Dorin Park School in September 1986 at the tender age of two and a half years. Alicia arrived with a big personality and a determination to be noticed. Alicia has a tremendous sense of fun and a great sense of humour. Alicia can keep you amused and on the edge of your seat with all sorts of stories…what she has done, where she has been, who she has met, and after half an hour or so, you may venture with the question of "Is this true, Alicia?" and she will respond with a glint in her eye and an enormous smile, "Of course it isn't." When Alicia smiles, she does it with her whole body, a smile that can't be missed.

It is a wicked sense of humour and her smile that will always attract your attention – and attention it attracts. Take Alicia anywhere, the Trafford Centre, Manchester Airport…wherever, she will always have half an eye out for a good-looking lad and somehow or other with a fluttering of the eyelids and a sideways glance, they will fall for it every time. Leave Alicia for only a few seconds and she will be engaging a good-looking lad in conversation.

Alicia knows her own mind and this is clear when it comes to fashion. She prides herself in being a fashion guru, knowing what is what and what suits. In a school with Speech Therapy, Physiotherapy and Occupational Therapy on tap, the area we have dramatically let Alicia down on is 'Retail Therapy' – Alicia loves shopping! In the heat of the day with everyone sweltering, Alicia will have her wrap-around Ray-Ban shades on and will look as cool as a cucumber. As fresh as a mountain spring, she will glide into a classroom, complete with shades but removing both sides of the door frame! Alicia has made many friends while at Dorin Park and Kurt remains a firm favourite. In fact, the wheelchairs are colour co-ordinated – Kurt in kingly red and Alicia with her royal blue insert. They lord overall at lunchtime in the yard!

**One of Alicia's real achievements is the writing and publishing of her very own poem book. Her poetry has the ability to amuse, entertain, inspire and move, a real tribute to her patience and imagination.**

Alicia is leaving Dorin Park to attend Yale College. I am sure Alicia will win friends with her humour and imagination. From all at Dorin Park, we wish Alicia the very best because she deserves the best.

Reading these comments again, I remember the very fun day we had at Manchester Airport. One of the officials asked one of our teachers if we were all getting on a plane. She was looking at her files very anxiously! It was so funny we laughed about it all the way back to school.

Coming back to my poetry book, having it published made me feel proud and clever. Writing the poetry book made me feel extremely proud.

When my book of poems was published, I asked family and friends to write their own poetry if my book had inspired them. I was surprised and very pleased to receive a poem from my uncle Barry. Uncle Barry is my Mum's younger brother. When you first meet him you'd think he is a quiet man.

Uncle Brian is the elder brother and he is very adventurous and still goes on holiday with his old motorbike friends, but it was Uncle Barry who wrote and sent me his poem. This is the poem he sent me.

## Alicia's Inspiration to Uncle Barry

My garden, it is very long.
The trees all grow big and strong.
Apples grow with mistletoe.
You must mind where your feet go!

I race along in my wheelchair.
Get in my way if you dare!

I had a dog her name was Blod,
A spotty dog but that's not odd.
A dalmatian you see was in her breed.
She helped me in my hours of need.
But sadly she has passed away.
She's gone to Heaven where she can play.

I have a Grampy. His name is Billy.
I know this sounds rather silly.
He's only five years older than me.
How on earth can that be?
It cannot be. The cries I hear,
But yes, he was born in a leap year!

I am your uncle. My name is Barry.
I read your poems and was as happy as Larry.
I set about some poems to write,
All very dark in the middle of the night.
Your poems nearly made me weep.
I'm knackered now so off to sleep.

I remember this poem from Uncle Barry arrived at our house on a little piece of paper, and poor Mum and I had to work out what Uncle Barry had written!

The other method of communication I used was the DynaVox. I persevered with DynaVox for a number of years. I got very little help from NHS speech therapists. I enrolled into Yale College Wrexham. Once again, the staff were unable to use DynaVox. So due to my inability to communicate, I had to leave sometime later.

I heard from a friend that there was a new eye gaze device that allows people with limited speech or hand movements to communicate. People were experimenting in ways with technology that could help people like me with cerebral palsy.

A speech-generating device changes the written words into spoken ones, and then into sentences and stories. My eye gaze equipment is more advanced than the earlier manually operated devices I had used in school and college.

I got my eye gaze from Smartbox Technology.

I have waited for a communication aid like this all my life. It's been a life-changer for me. It's been the best thing for my communication with family and friends. I've had it for five years now. I can now have my say and say it how I want.

I learnt how to use it very quickly. I'm so proud. Family and friends have had a go but find it too hard to use. I find it easy!

And now I can write this book.

Having this eye gaze aid has made a huge difference in my life. My first sentence on it was, "How are you today, Mum, Dad? I'm fine."

Some days later I said to Mum and Dad,

"Have I been a burden to you all these years?"

Mum said, "Of course you haven't. I don't know what we'd have done without you."

You can see the photo of me communicating on this eye gaze. I'm using my eyes to talk.

# Chapter Four
## Listen to My Voice

I've got a brain like you have. I also have feelings.

Communication is a major problem for me. Family and friends cope very well as they understand the different ways I have to get things over to them. Initially, body language plays a big part. Then Grampy taught me to demonstrate the alphabet numerically using my hands to show the letters, for example, one means A. After this, communication aids played a big part. My current eye gaze equipment makes things a whole lot easier. However, it is not always possible to take the eye gaze around with me and I have to resort to the old methods. All I ask is for patience and understanding.

Also, please talk to me not my companions.

I have found myself in many situations where I have felt insulted with people talking down to me as if I was a baby. They see the chair not me.

Coming back from holiday, checking in at the airport, two smartly dressed middle-aged women began talking to us. They asked Mum and Dad lots of questions about me. In a very loud voice, one of them asked, "Have you had her sterilised?"

My Dad replied, "No, we've had her pasteurised."

I burst out laughing. Luckily the two of them walked off leaving most of the other people in the queue scandalised.

We were in a hotel in Spain and Mum was feeding me. Another holidaymaker watching Mum feeding me said,

"Is she blind?"

"Why do you ask that?" Mum said.

"I thought she was blind because you were feeding her."

Here's a great one. We went to Warrington to see an exhibition of equipment for the disabled. You had to have a ticket to get in. When two young girls weren't allowed in because they didn't have tickets they took their annoyance out on me. First, they used these gestures implying that I should have been walking. Then they said in loud voices,

"I bet she can walk."

Mum was so angry. She said to the two girls, "How dare you? Be careful. You might end up in a wheelchair yourself."

In 2001, a group of us went to Disneyland in Paris with Miles of Smiles. You had to be nominated to go.

One of my friends, Hayley went. Hayley was very bright and could speak fluent French. All of us who went were disabled. We were sitting in a group together. A group of French students were staring at us very rudely. Hayley walked towards them with a camera and in perfect French asked them would they like to take a photograph of us all.

"Vous voudriez prendre une photo de nous tous?"

At least they all looked ashamed and had the sense to stop staring at us.

While I don't like people being unpleasant to me, I dislike it even more when people are sorry for me.

When people show that they are sorry for me, it makes me feel upset with my life.

When we go out for meals, I find Italian waiters are the best. They are patient. They give me time to pick what I want, give me time to look at the menu, to look at the menu without them pointing at it.

"Take your time," they say.

They are good at understanding disability and know how to work with it like they make sure we've got the right table, a high table for my wheelchair. They even have time to make jokes about the weather!

Last year when I was at the zoo, a couple came up to me and asked my carer, not me, "Would she like some smarties?"

I was really cross. Me and Katie though just burst out laughing.

When I go shopping in the town with my family and friends, the shop assistant talks to other people who are there rather than to me. "Does she like it?" they say as if I wasn't there. Dad is the worst to be with.

He will always say, "Ask her yourself".

I like it though when he sticks up for me.

The worse thing is restaurants. I can point to the menu and show what food I want but the waiter will talk to each individual and not to me. They always ask other people what I want. They say, "Does she need a menu?" Don't they know that I can read?

Even more insulting: "Does she want her meal blended?" they ask my family or friends. I feel like punching someone. I like going to a certain Italian restaurant that we've found. The waiters treat me differently. They have patience and time and wait for me.

Here's some of the other patronising things that have been said to me:

Ah, bless her! Is she blind? patting me on the head.

Does she want some sweeties?

Ah! She's cute.

Can I talk to you?

Why are you in a wheelchair?

Yes, I know what you're saying.

Are you happy today?

Do you understand me?


People feeling sorry for me and talking to my Mum and carers and not to me:

LISTEN TO MY VOICE!

# Chapter Five
## Happy Memories: Work

At school, communication was better, although mostly using the old methods, like Makaton. Technology did not catch up until the latter end of my school time. After leaving school, I tried to further my education by attending college. This was a disaster, due to the staff having no understanding of my modern equipment or any of my old methods of communication. I felt I was let down very badly.

The last year at school we would visit local colleges for an afternoon. This system was recommended by those in education. There was a choice of day colleges or we could choose a residential college. I wanted to stay near home and go to a day college as I had other activities I liked to go to in my own area. I chose a college then that was just a short drive away from where I lived. It was the worst choice to make but unknown to me at the time.

The personal carer who had been selected by my school was going to support me at college. Great! But two weeks before I enrolled at college she had to back out because of personal reasons. So then when I started at the college, the support carer that the college had picked for me was not trained to understand my disability, my communication needs, my personal care, so I had many different helpers who didn't have a clue. Not one was able to use communication aids. I was using at that time DynaVox. I was told to try to use the computer but without the special switch I needed. I got very angry and frustrated as the weeks went by. On one occasion, I banged my fist on the table with the stress of it all. I was sent to see the Principal to be reprimanded for my actions. They sent for my parents to pick me up. Mum was upset. She said I cried that day. I tried to explain that I felt like I was the carer, not the support workers that they had chosen for me. I remember one not even bothering to take her coat off all day and she kept her handbag on her shoulder as if she was waiting to leave at any moment!

The outcome was that they gave me no choice but to leave. The very last meeting we had with the staff from the special needs department in the college was very unhelpful. One of the teachers recommended that I see a doctor to be put on medication. They didn't think that they were in the wrong. We left the meeting absolutely disgusted.

We did put in a complaint to the college. The college just reminded us of 'the incident' that had happened when I had lost my temper. At a later date, we went to Dial House on another issue and we told them what had happened at college. We had been told about the Disability Discrimination Law that was passed in 1995 and updated in 2010. When Mum and Dad discussed my ordeal at college with Dial House, Mum and Dad were told they had left it too late to complain as over six months had passed since the incident.

Much later on after leaving college, I was introduced to a group of voluntary workers. I successfully applied to join them. The group leaders and other members were keen for me to use whatever method of communication was necessary, including my high-tech gear. My life improvement was tremendous.

When I was twenty-five, I met up with my friend Celyn. She told me about a job working in a voluntary group in Wrexham for social services. At the time my support worker was my good friend Heulwen. We were both keen to join the group.

I did the job for four years.

The clients we worked with were in supported living houses. Four people lived in each house. Each had different disabilities. Some were wheelchair users. Some had mental health issues. I was given my house to visit once a week with my carer Heulwen. We would sit down, have a cup of tea, and talk to each client on their own to see what help was needed. It was good to make it a social visit, not racing in and out, but sitting down and giving plenty of time to listen carefully. Mostly the problems were about the difficulties of living together, sorting out differences at mealtimes, things about each other that came across as annoying. I think that because I am disabled, the clients found it easier to tell me their problems. I wouldn't patronise them. Disabled people can offer a special understanding of others' needs. We can have insight into others' problems.

Once a month, all the volunteer group met together in a local pub to socialise together. Some of the clients were very vulnerable and had to be supported and looked after. I remember that when I went to the pub I didn't do too much socialising. I was too busy making sure one of the very vulnerable clients was OK and not being exploited!

In the voluntary group was Paula, 'the boss', as she liked to call herself, and there were ten of us other volunteers. Apart from Paula, all the group had some kind of disability. This gave us an understanding of different disabilities and the challenges that are faced as disabled adults. Over time we built up friendships with the service users. They looked forward to us coming.

The group worked really well together. We had our meetings once or twice a week. Sometimes it was hard but I liked it a lot. It was called Supported Living. When we visited the houses and homes of service users with all different disabilities, we would help them fill in forms or ask if they were happy with their present situation. What I used for work was my DynaVox. I used my DynaVox with prepared questions. Were they getting all their needs met? Then we would take any information back to the group of ten. At the meetings, we would discuss and try to solve any problems going on and make an action plan. The group was very good and understanding.

I also did some interviewing for new staff which I loved doing. It was so interesting.

I felt like I was a very important part of the group when we worked together. My ideas were a very important part in the group and were listened to. Did I make friends with anyone in the group? Oh yeah!

Typical meeting:

"Have you got any gossip this week, Paula?"

"Are we doing any work today?"

I would have to say that just to shut them up as for the first forty five minutes they would just spend gossiping about the week they'd had.

They would still be chatting at lunchtime if I hadn't have stopped them. I would have to say, "Are we doing anything to do with work today?"

"OK Alicia!"

And then they would get to work.

I was good at my job. I was curious about all the information and the service users we met. Our group was so good and we met so many people.

We were presented with an award for our work which we received from the Welsh assembly in Cardiff. We were all ecstatic to receive the prestigious award for our group of volunteers. It was an award for working with people with disabilities.

It was a big day. We were all dressed up. I had a nice red dress on. I thought on the day that I looked really nice. I still have the dress now.

We were on our way to Cardiff in a taxi. My Mum said it was the worst journey of her life. She said the taxi driver seemed to think he was on a racetrack! One of the passengers was sick, three carrier bags of sick. Horrible, smelly taxi. It was a nightmare. I thought it was really funny and couldn't stop laughing. Even thinking about it now makes me laugh.

The award-giving took place in the town hall in Cardiff. The hall was amazing. It was really big and it was packed. On the stage were the awards that were to be given out. All the VIPs of Social Services were seated. Celyn was chosen to go up to the stage to get our trophy. As she went up, Paula began to cry, then Mum began to cry, then we all began to cry! There was a standing ovation. The clapping went on for five minutes. It was great. And the refreshments, lots of nice nibbles, were great too!

We had people serving us refreshments. We felt so important.

How do you think I felt then when one of the best times in my life came to an end?

I was unfortunately ill for three months. For personal reasons, I was absent from work for a while, and when I went back, we had a back-to-work meeting where I was told that because there had been a change in council regulations, I couldn't work there as I lived out of the designated area. I was very upset and again felt let down. I was expecting them to say I could return. I was very confused, disappointed and low. I felt upset every day for quite a while. I didn't think I would ever get over it. Yes, that's what I thought at the time.

When we enquired about the decision for me to leave the job, we were asked to go for a meeting with the Head of the Department to discuss their decision. The building where we went for the meeting was massive. We had to get to the office down a long, long corridor. The Head of Department was very friendly. She offered us a cup of coffee. She chatted away asking me questions. Had I liked the job? What had I liked best? She had heard that I'd been very good at the job. I began to feel really hopeful. Mum and Dad began to feel hopeful. Then she said that I had to give up the job. We were very shocked and so disappointed.

Dad said, "Why did you bring us all this way knowing you were going to say no? Why didn't you just tell us in a letter?"

I felt so low. Going back down that long, long corridor was a terrible experience.

At first, I couldn't meet up with the people I'd worked with. I found it too upsetting. Then I started meeting up again with Paula.

I think I should have a job in this life.

I'm glad though I was part of the group. I'm sorry it all came to an end but I feel proud that I've done it.

I thought writing about work would be hard but it hasn't been. Happy memories.

# Chapter Six
## Where Feathers Are Near Loved Ones Appear: My Family

We are an extended family as Mum and Dad have both been married before. Mum had two boys, Simon and Stuart. Dad had two girls, Karen and Lesley, and one boy Peter. Then I came along as a big surprise! Mum said I was the icing on the cake. Simon and Stuart were at home with me. Karen, Lesley and Peter had flown the nest but never went far from home. We had many birthdays and Christmases together. There was always fun and laughter and I was treated no differently than my brothers and sisters.

I wrote this poem about our Christmases together.

## Christmas Eve

Happy smiling faces,
Noses rosy red,
Children full of excitement
Before they go to bed.

Santa will be busy,
Lots of presents in his
sack.
Goodbye Mr Robin.
I'll be back later for a chat.

A log fire is awaiting
And mince pies at the ready,
Only the fairy on the tree
Calls out to Rudolph to be steady.
The snow is gently falling
On the rooftop overnight.
A snowman in the garden
Will soon be a beautiful sight.

Christmas morning has arrived,
Turkey roast and Christmas pud,
Crackers, baubles, tinsel,
Just look at everything.
Isn't it good?

Going out for meals has always been a great opportunity for a family get-together. We always celebrate birthdays or special occasions, or just have a meal together when we meet up. Sometimes it's just girls night out together. We like to try different restaurants. We've found some really good restaurants and pubs that will take our dog, Lottie. Lottie is really good. She sits under the table through all the courses, not moving until Mum puts on her coat. Then she starts barking, knowing at last, it's time to go home.

"Does she want a treat?" the waiter says.

Lottie would rather sit for hours under the table being with her family than being at home on her own.

I wrote this poem about Lottie!

**My Dog Lottie**
My dog Lottie
Runs in front of bike riders,
Sits on the bed,
Sits on the settee for a tickle
On her tummy.
Fussy eater,
Only likes chicken!
Dances on her back legs
Like a small child.
I love her a lot.
My dog Lottie.

Simon and Stuart loved football and they both played for local teams so the house was always full of boys in their football gear. Quite a lot of girls used to call as well! My brothers were very good looking and handsome!

Dad worked abroad most of the time. He could be away for six weeks at a time, then home for two or three weeks. Then we would plan a family holiday.

My very first holiday with Mum and Dad was in Paris. I was just six months old. Our first family holiday was on my first birthday. Thirteen of us went to Portugal. We had to have two villas. On the plane, we opened my cards and presents and all the passengers on the plane sang happy birthday to me, so I've been told.

One year, Simon and Stuart and their friends went to Greece on holiday. While there they met up with a group of girls from Glasgow. Simon kept in touch with one of the girls, Geraldine. The rest is history. It was a holiday romance. They married and had three beautiful children, Joe, Jamie and Katie. My nephew, Joe, is very artistic. He is currently in the sixth form at school and he is hoping to progress to specialist art college.

He is the tallest member of my family. He likes wearing these big boots. He likes them but I'm not too sure. He is bubbly, clever, out-going. His technology skills are exceptional. He likes to live life to the full. Sport is not at the top of his list, quite the opposite of Jamie.

Jamie, what can I say? Football mad. Every Summer holiday, they come to stay for a week. Jamie is full of fun and always going on about his football. He supports Liverpool like me. Mum supports Liverpool too.

Dad supports Manchester United!

Each time I see Jamie he's got a new kit!

Here is a poem I wrote about him.

## My Nephew Jamie

My nephew Jamie likes to be on the go.
He has more energy than anyone I know.
Football is his favourite game.
But he's as good at dancing as
the kids in Fame.
Swimming came way down on
his list.

But now when Friday comes, he
won't give it a miss.
He had a shot at judo for a
while,
But then he needed something
else to make him smile.
What about table tennis? he was
asked.
He said he had never played but
he was a blast!
The latest we have heard along with all his other sports
Is none other than horse riding of course!
But football is his favourite game.
I look forward to hearing people say
Did you see your Jamie on Match of the Day?

Katie is very good fun and outgoing. She just graduated in teaching and is doing very well. She adores Chester Zoo and has to visit every year even at twenty-two. I think one of her favourite memories in life so far is getting to wash the elephants in Thailand. Katie likes this poem I wrote about her when she was just a little girl.

## Katie Ann My Niece

Katie Ann is my niece.
She calls a sandwich a piece!
She thinks she's ten
But she's really four.
She looks funny
When she stands tall.
She loves colouring
In her book,
Katie Ann my funny little niece!

When Simon met Geraldine, she was doing a teacher's degree. When she graduated, she decided to go into special needs teaching, I guess because of me.

Mum recently found this lovely piece of writing that Geraldine had written about me.

## My Sister-in-Law Alicia

I first met Alicia on my first trip to Chester to visit her brother Simon when she was just five years old. She was a very cute little girl with really blonde hair and big browny-hazel eyes and she also had something called cerebral palsy.

I had never met anyone with cerebral palsy before and even when her brother told me that his sister had cerebral palsy, I wasn't really sure what it was and I was too embarrassed to ask!

On that first Saturday afternoon in October in 1989 sitting in the kitchen, Alicia's Mum, Brenda, asked her what she wanted on her sandwich, jam or honey. I remember thinking why are you asking her that, she won't know what you mean and she won't be able to tell  you. I didn't think Alicia could understand or communicate. Then Alicia's brother, Simon said, "Right, whose knee do you want to sit on?"

And before I knew it, Alicia was sitting in my lap. I was very embarrassed as I had no idea how to speak to Alicia or what to say! I began to speak to her as if she were a baby because I really thought she could not understand me.

How wrong I was!

The more I got to know Alicia, I very quickly realised that she was a very bright little girl with great imagination and a wicked sense of humour. We used to spend hours in her bedroom playing with the hundreds of dolls and teddies she had. I can still remember some of them…Pound Puppy, Jogging Bear, Piggly Wiggly. We had great fun!

I developed a keen interest in cerebral palsy and when I had to choose a topic for my final research assignment, I decided to research cerebral palsy and how to teach cerebral palsy children. Alicia was my inspiration for this as I will always remember what I first thought of people with cerebral palsy, and it's probably what a lot of other people think too. I wanted to learn so I could pass the knowledge on to these people.

When I finished my degree, I was very excited about starting my first teaching post, but what was even more exciting was that I had landed a teaching post in a school for children with cerebral palsy. I spent four years in that school and in that time, I learned so much about cerebral palsy, the different types of cerebral palsy and the vast differences in how it affects children. However, the most important thing I learned was that what all of the children had in common was that they were children who like to play, laugh and learn just like other children.

Alicia has had many, many achievements in her life and I am so pleased that I have been part of her family to share some of those special moments from watching her learn to crawl so that she could choose the room she wanted to be in, to her writing some beautiful poems about her brothers and niece.

Achievements that are special to Simon and I are the day she was our bridesmaid and became my sister-in-law. Also, how wonderful an Aunty she is to our children Katie and Joseph and our niece Holly. The special bond she has with them all is wonderful. I think her job as Aunty is one she does very well indeed but I also know she has  many, many achievements ahead of her and these will make us even more proud of her than we are today!

I always knew Simon would be a great Dad. He was so helpful when my Dad was away. If I had one of my seizures, I would know it was his voice and it would keep me calm.

Stuart missed Simon a lot when he moved to Scotland as they were very close brothers. Not long after Simon left home, Stuart met Nicky. She soon became part of the family. Stuart and Nicky both looked after the house when we went to live in Dubai for a year, where Dad was working at the time.

When we came home, Stuart and Nicky decided to move into a flat. After a few years, they saved enough to buy a house. Three years later along came baby Holly.

There was great excitement as Simon and Geraldine were expecting their second baby at the same time. Simon and Stuart were just as close as ever up and down to Scotland and enjoying many holidays together.

The year I was twenty-one and Holly was four and a half, ready to go into full-time school, Stuart and Nicky decided to get married.

Simon and the family and many of their friends came down for the wedding. Stuart and Nicky had lots of friends who were invited. They were a very popular couple, and Holly made a beautiful flower girl.

The wedding was absolutely amazing. Stuart and Nicky looked so happy, the perfect couple.

Off they went on their honeymoon. We looked after Holly as she was used to staying with Nan and Grandad and Aunt

Alicia. Mum had been looking after Holly since she was five months old while Nicky was working.

The second week they were away, Holly went to stay with Uncle Simon and Auntie Geraldine in Scotland.

Three days after they came back from their honeymoon, Stuart was on his way to work on his bike as usual, when he had a cardiac arrest.

He was rushed to hospital but he never survived. He died on the way to hospital after the medics fought to save him. I don't remember much. It was all a blur and happened so fast, but it was a Wednesday morning and Mum's friend called to say Stuart had fallen off his bike. So Dad rushed down the road to see if he was OK. Mum and I waited at home to hear some news. Mum was in a panic, pacing up and down. Then the phone rang. It was Nicky, Stuart's wife, with the sad news. Mum was screaming. I just knew.

It was the saddest day of our lives. Just three weeks after his beautiful wedding, and they were meant to be picking Holly up in two days.

He had the biggest personality ever.

He lit up a room.

He was the funniest person you could meet.

He was the loveliest Daddy to Holly.

He was my dearest brother.
He loved music like no one else.
He was loved by all who knew him.


I'll always remember a funny story about Stuart and his best mate Dale who were inseparable. They were Liverpool football fans. Before a match started, they would phone each other to talk about the game, then at half time they would chat again, and as soon as it was the final whistle, they would ring again whatever the score, that's if they couldn't get tickets for the game!

Dale is still a very big part of our lives.

My Mum was strong. She said, "I put my grief on hold because I was grieving for his wife Nicky, his brother Simon and his sister Alicia and of course his beautiful daughter, Holly."

Holly is a loud person in my family and has a big personality. Holly likes to talk all the time and you can't get a word in edgeways when she is around. If I'm not sure about something she is very friendly and has a great understanding of me and will help me. When you feel like sleeping, she will always have some event or drama to tell you about, then you're wide awake and can't sleep.

She is great at swimming very fast in the water and very dedicated. She will go training five mornings a week starting at six o'clock in the morning. She is very hardworking and will go far in life. Her Dad would be very proud. Don't think he would like the fact she has started dating but that's another story.

My family has always been very important to me.

I always feel safe when Dad's around. He tells me that he's sorry that he was away working so many years of my life, but it was always exciting when I knew he was on his way home. He would tell me great stories of all the different places he had worked or been.

My Dad would tell me great stories. I loved the stories he told me about Kuwait. I went there in 1988 when I was there for a month's vacation, but I don't remember much about it. Dad told me we stayed in this great apartment that had its own swimming pool, barbecue, bowling alley and our own maid called Sebastian. Mum says she was only young and came to meet us with her mother. She had her own room and she loved helping to look after me. We loved going to a restaurant that was a converted galleon. Dad told me Saddam Hussain was something of a hero then and was always on the television. One scary story is that we had gone to the fish market in Shuwaik Port and a bomb had gone off. It was the time of the Gulf War between Iran and Iraq.

When we could, Mum and I would go and stay with him if where he was working was accessible for my wheelchair and my special needs.

Dad and I love quizzes but Dad always wins! He's a very knowledgeable person. He's very caring and a good organiser. He's a big soft teddy!

My Mum is so special to me. Here's one of the many poems I have written about my Mum.

**My Mum**

My Mum is easy to love.
She is my best friend.
She makes me happy when I feel sad.
She looks after me and my Dad.
My Mum loves talking on the phone.
She likes shopping for new clothes.
I think her cooking is great.
She makes a fuss of all the family
But hates anyone to be late!
My Mum can understand me
When I don't say a word.
People ask her how she can know.
She says it's in her head, not her toe!
My Mum is easy to love.

We enjoy doing lots of things together like shopping!

## I Like Shopping

I like shopping,
So does my Mum.
Anyone who doesn't
Must be dumb!
In and out of the shops we go
Spending our money to and
fro.
Mum bought a dress.
I bought some pants
 But, on our list,
Were garden plants!
"Shall we stop for a coffee?"
says Mum.

"I'd rather have pop and a sticky bun."

Yes, my Mum is so special to me. We are the best of friends. Since the day I was born she has had to do everything for me. Without any complaints, she gets me out of bed, washes me, cleans my teeth, dries my hair, feeds me, helps me into my wheelchair, with fun and laughter. I love it when she dances around the kitchen when one of her favourite songs is playing on the radio.

My Mum is a great cook, always trying new recipes out on me and Dad. She is very artistic. Her amazing paintings are all over the house. She doesn't realise how clever she is.

It took Mum a long time to admit she needed help with the everyday routine with looking after me. She said it was her job but now I have two amazing carers who are also my friends. Thanks to my beautiful Mum.

Yes, my family is very important to me.

Families are important to everyone.

My family has given me understanding.

We are always planning. What are we going to do today? The best thing about my family is that we stick together.

# Chapter Seven
## Travels

Travel plays a big part in my family life. We have travelled a lot over the years. We like going around churches and cathedrals. I love the high ceilings in cathedrals and how old than older they are! Before we travel, careful planning must be carried out. Accommodation, air, sea and road travel are top of the list and general accessibility. Each location has to be considered. We have coped well with good and bad situations. We try to put the bad ones aside and remember the good ones with pleasure.

We first went to France I'm told, when I was only six months old so I don't remember much! I love Mum and Dad telling me though that we stayed in a lovely hotel close to the Paris city centre. Apparently, we visited all the famous landmarks, Notre Dame, the Eiffel Tower, Arc de Triomphe, and took a boat trip on the Seine, and went to beautiful parks and gardens. Before we left for home Mum and Dad said we'd come again so I must have enjoyed it!

Our next visit to France was many years later. This time we stayed in a lovely villa near Coutances in Normandy. We flew to Paris and hired a car driving cross country to Normandy. The countryside was breath-taking. Our main reason for visiting Normandy was to remember the turning point in World War Two. My Grandfather fought with the Royal Artillery throughout the battle of Normandy.

Unfortunately, he was killed in Holland in September the same year. Later in the year, we plan to visit Geel in Belgium. Because my Grandfather was killed in the second world war, we try to visit his grave as often as possible to pay our respects.

It was very moving visiting the famous D Day landing beaches. We paid our respects to the fallen at the US war cemetery above Omaha beach and the Commonwealth war graves in Bayeux. While we were in Bayeux, we took a trip to the city museum where the Bayeux tapestry is on view. We also visited the city of Caen where there is a beautiful modern museum called Le Memorial dedicated to the liberation of France.

The countryside in Normandy is beautiful. It's hard to believe how badly it was destroyed during the war. The coastline heading towards St Malo is lovely. We took a trip down the coast from Coutances to Mount St Michel. We shopped on the way at Granville where we were tempted to take the local ferry to Jersey but didn't have time. Another trip.

Another trip was to the famous cathedral in Lisieux. This is the home of St Theresa. Theresa is Mum's confirmation name and the name of our local church at home. Our two weeks in

Normandy were soon over. Another place we'll visit again. We returned to Le Charles de Gaulle airport for our flight home reminding ourselves we still haven't returned to Paris as promised. We did finally make it to Paris in 2014. We went after my thirtieth birthday party.

I'll never forget how we were allowed to go halfway up the Eiffel Tower. We could go no further due to limited access for my wheelchair. However, even at this level, it felt like I was on the top of the whole city.

We went to Notre Dame which was breath-taking. I hadn't realised it was on an island. It is one of the biggest cathedrals I have been in and the most beautiful.

We took a boat ride on the river Seine. It was good for sightseeing. We went to see the Arc de Triomphe, the second most famous landmark. The view of the Champs-Elysees is amazing.

The food was good! And we found a perfect accommodation for me right in the middle of Paris.

I remember well the second time we visited Rome. We stayed in a fantastic hotel that was previously owned by the Vatican. The surrounding grounds and gardens were amazing.

There were huge statues in white marble and giant pots everywhere with unusual flowers in them. The staff were especially friendly towards us. We had a really big room with a large bathroom and walk-in shower – all accessible for my wheelchair. One of the Italian waiters made a great fuss over

me each time we went into the restaurant for breakfast or evening meals. He would always pick the right table for me to feel comfortable. One evening, he wanted to know why I was all dressed up in my new dress. My Mum told him it was my birthday and he said I looked beautiful, in his lovely broken English. He then asked if he could have a photo with me.

After that photo, you can imagine my face! Later, he surprised me with a special pudding. That was the highlight of my holiday. I will always remember that birthday in Rome.

Another favourite holiday was our visit to Valencia. It has the biggest aquarium in the world. The river had dried up in the centre of the city and it is now a huge park. We stayed in a high-rise apartment on the top floor, the fifteenth floor! We used to count all the floors, all fifteen of them as we went up and down! It had a large balcony overlooking the sea. We would walk along the beach every day. It stretched for miles. Looking out from our apartment we used to watch people exercising their horses on the beach. The horses loved the sand and the sea. We would walk to the city and back. It was cooler in the morning. That's one thing I do remember.

We've only been to Malta once but what a memorable holiday. A couple of days into the holiday we met up with some lovely people. Each day, I would go into the pool either before or after we went sight-seeing. The older couple of the people we met with came from Mansfield. The guy, Alf was his name, would come over to talk to us, and he wanted to know all about me. He said it made him feel happy watching me come out of my wheelchair and go straight into the pool splashing with a big smile on my face. John, from the other couple that we were friendly with and who came from Ireland, one day decided to join me in the pool. He said his girlfriend didn't like swimming. She just liked sunbathing. So we, John and I, used to have great fun in the pool. He always asked Mum and Dad's permission to play games with me in the pool. One day he took me down a huge slide. Mum's face was a picture of shock but I loved it. Then it became a competition;

who do I swim with today, John or Alf? I mostly chose John because he was younger and stronger!

We used to all meet together in the evening for food and drinks and a chat about what we had done that day.

We were going home before John and Susanne, his partner. John said he would get up early to say his goodbyes. Most nights John and Susanne would go to a club until the early hours so we didn't expect to see John the next morning to say our goodbyes. But yes, he was there! We were all very emotional. John was full of tears, so was I, and Mum was too. John said, "Who will I have to play with in the pool? I will miss you!"

We have been to so many places. Canada was one of my favourites. We spent two weeks there. We went on a boat trip on Maid of The Mist to see the Niagara Falls. We went under the falls. Wonderful. We stayed four days in Toronto, three days in Niagara and a week in a log cabin on Rice Lake. We visited CN Tower and almost got to the top but unfortunately, the last few feet were not accessible but really, we were high enough. There was a glass panel in the floor and Mum took her photos through the glass panel floor! We saw the Jersey Boys in the  theatre on Yonge Street. We did consider walking to the theatre but we were told Yonge Street is eight miles long! We drove from Niagara across Toronto to Rice Lake near the town of Peterborough. We needed a chill-out week just to relax!

We have been to America three times.

We have been to many, many places in Spain.

We have taken many holidays abroad and our latest plans are to visit Marbella in Spain. We have been kindly given the use of a friend's apartment and are looking forward to trying out the resort. We have visited before, but only for day trips when staying in other locations in southern Spain.

We've been to Portugal four times. We visit Belgium every two years. We've been just the once to Ireland and Germany but we visit Holland regularly. We visit art galleries, museums and cathedrals both in Belgium and Holland. I always enjoyed day trips to Bruges, Antwerp and Eindhoven. We've even been to Lapland to see Father Christmas and enjoy a sleigh ride with the huskies and reindeer!

One of my many happy memories was going to Lourdes on a pilgrimage each year at Easter. I was first nominated by my Mum's Auntie Mary, to travel with a group called Flame. Flame is a Catholic  organisation and takes children and adults with different disabilities from the North West of England to the Holy Site in Lourdes during the Easter holidays. Over the years I have been to Lourdes five times, four with Mum and once with a Flame volunteer called Karen. One day I hope to make another visit to Lourdes as we must take Dad for a holiday there.

Visits to the Holy Shrine of St. Bernadette, the Holy Grotto of the Virgin Mary, and the Basilica, will remain with me for the rest of my life. It was in Lourdes I took my first holy communion and confirmation. I chose Bernadette as my confirmation name. I was five years old when I first heard the story of Bernadette. I chose the name Bernadette because I was so intrigued by the story of Bernadette's life. It was my first choice. Bernadette was a very sickly child but she had a really strong faith. That to me was the most important part of the pilgrimage to Lourdes to go to the holy grotto where Bernadette had seen the Virgin Mary. I had the opportunity to bathe in the ice-cold waters. It takes your breath away. During our pilgrimages, we met people from all over the world. The experience of the trip is emotional and enlightening and brings inner peace. While there we have made many lifelong friends. I first thought it would be sad to see people with severe disabilities, but it was so inspirational to see so many happy smiley faces, mine included. I will always be so grateful to Sister Gertie, Bishop Tom and all the Flame volunteers. While we were at Lourdes, Martin, who played the guitar during Mass, put together two of my poems, made them into a song and set the song to music. When we got back to Britain, we were invited to a special mass at a church in Liverpool to celebrate my eighteenth birthday. I was given a beautiful bouquet of flowers, and best of all, the song of my poems was sung during the mass. It was very emotional. My Mum was crying and so were my brother and sister-in-law. The church was full.

Here are the two poems that Martin made into a song and set to music.

### Myself

I use a wheelchair
Because I can't walk.
I use a voice box
Because I can't talk.
I listen to people.
I take it all in.
Some look surprised when I have a big grin.

I write on my computer
Stories I like to tell.
People like to read them
And it's helping me to spell!
My family call me 'clever clogs'
When they read my poems.
It helps me to express my thoughts
And my mind that roams.

## Joy

Joy is a happy feeling.
Joy is hope.
Joy can be colourful.
Joy is being with someone special.
Joy is birthdays and Christmas rolled into one.
Joy is giving.
Joy is winning.
Joy is helping.
Joy is chocolate and ribs and chips.

We currently take later vacations. At home, we have found great self-catering cottages in Cornwall, Conway and Blackpool. All cater very well for my disability and we can also take our lovely dog, Lottie. We enjoy long walks in the countryside and along the coast.

I think it's really sad when those people with a disability don't want to go travelling. It's best to find out before you go that the situations you'll be involved with will be OK. And even if there are problems, you can always try to fix them. Mum always makes sure we're all right even if it means changing all the furniture around! She always puts everything back in place though before we leave!

Travelling gives you more insight into the world around you.

# Chapter Eight
## My Achievements

When I was seven, I joined the Brownies. It was a really friendly group. Everyone got on well and I was a valued member of the group. I was treated no differently to any of the other girls. I had to memorise the vows too. Brown Owl was lovely. We used to go camping.

My favourite bit was singing around the fire before we went to bed. Then when I was ten or eleven, I moved up to Girl Guides until I was sixteen. What I remember very well was carrying the flag into Chester cathedral on Remembrance Sunday. I was wearing the uniform, the hat and everything else. The flag was attached to my wheelchair and I held onto the pole. This was very special to me in every way. Mum and Dad were so proud and moved. Dad especially was very emotional.

After leaving school finding further education was a problem. College as I've said had been a big disappointment. When I was about twenty years old, my support worker at this time was a young lady called Donna. She had heard of an organisation called Learn Direct, who were closely associated with the University of Chester and Liverpool. I enrolled for a literacy course which lasted for about a year. I did the course with Learn Direct through the Chester and Liverpool universities. It was a literature course. I managed to achieve a City and Guild grade three, the equivalent to a GCSE.

The time I spent at Learn Direct was a great success. I rated it ten out of ten. Before I started the course, I did an IQ test on the computer. I scored quite highly.

I was quite surprised to get City and Guild awards. I got lots of awards that proved how successful I'd been doing all the courses. It was the first time I had done something like this in my life. It was quite easy at the end of the day. I give it ten out of ten!

I would read a lot of book reviews and then pick a book with Mum's help. Then I would answer questions about the book I had last read. It was a test to see if I'd understood the book. I got top marks.

I especially liked books about myths and legends. *Arabian Nights* was a favourite. I liked using my imagination. I also, as you'll appreciate, loved poetry books. My very favourite book though is *Hitler Stole Pink Rabbit* by Judith Kerr. It is a great book about a very sad family in World War Two. The family has to travel around. The book was made into a television series last year. I think of it more though as a holiday book. We took it on holiday. We take a book with us every holiday for Mum and me to read together.

I also love books about astrology and astronomy. Because I liked astrology so much my lovely carer Vicky bought me a star on the anniversary of my brother Stuart's death. Another star was bought by Aunty Angela. These two stars were bought from a creative product called Name A Star. I called one star Stuart, after my brother, and the other star, Alicia. I've got two stars, Stuart and Alicia, up in the sky. From the map the company sent us, you can see where my stars are in the galaxy.

Vicky wrote a lovely letter to my mum.

**Brenda,**
**I have already registered the star for you. I thought it**
**would be a nice idea because of the song you love about**
**the stars.**
**Love Vicky**

The song Vicky mentions is *Waiting for a Star to Fall* by
the group Boy Meets Girl. Mum loves it. My sister-in-law
Nicky played it as the first song at Mum's seventieth birthday
party. Mum and Nicky danced to the song. Vicky was crying
all the way through the song.

Anyway, the time I spent at Learn Direct was a great
success. This is a quote from my ICT teacher.

**I think it is fair to say that Alicia has done brilliantly**
**up to date. Many literacy learners do not study level 2 at**
**all. They rarely work up to the level in as little time as**
**Alicia has done. She enjoys herself here and is treated the**
**same as all the other learners. In fact, she requires less**
**support than most learners due to the fact that she is**
**comfortable with the learning material.**

At that time, I was going to a centre called Canal Street.
The staff were very supportive and sent carers to support me
with the Learn Direct studies. I was very grateful and so was
the college. My ICT teacher wrote.

**We are grateful that Canal Street continues with**
**support with her as we cannot devote one-on-one time but**
**we do closely monitor her progress.**

I found it very rewarding at the end of the day, but
unfortunately, there was no follow on, and the Learn Direct
office has now closed and turned into a shop.

I'm very pleased that my Mum has kept all my certificates over the years. Looking back at them makes me feel very proud.

My only positive achievement for my time at our local further education college was from the art class. A part of the course was dedicated, for my benefit, to foot painting. I wasn't sure at first, but my tutor encouraged me to try, and to my surprise, I was quite good. I used my feet to paint by holding the paintbrush between my toes. I had my artwork displayed in the college. I painted a picture of a house surrounded by trees for my brother Stuart, and one of poppies for Mum and Dad. This has pride of place at home. That picture is still in Mum and Dad's bedroom. I give the painting with feet course ten out of ten. When the course ended, we tried to find some follow up, but unfortunately, the only courses available were in London. I would like to look into doing foot painting again.

Travel and leisure plays a big part in my life. Time to switch off and relax is very important. I have enjoyed some exciting achievements when I've been away from home.

We decided to go to Florida during Autumn 1997. We did the usual, Universal, Disney. To make the trip even more special I wanted to try something special. Swimming with dolphins was mentioned but due to health and safety restrictions, this was not possible. Then I saw an ad for a hot air balloon ride. Mum and Dad thought it would be out of the question. However, we made further enquiries and were told in a typical American style 'no problem', so on 1/10/97 I went on Orange Blossom hot air balloon in Florida with my Mum and Dad. We had to get up at five in the morning before the sunrise. A special hot air balloon was provided. The basket allowed the pilot, me in my wheelchair, and Mum and Dad. After initial safety checks were made, we were up in the air by 5.30-ish. The pilot was confident making me feel so comfortable. A larger balloon took off at the same time and we were both rising to a thousand feet. Photographs were exchanged between each group.

Up, up we went. We stayed in the air for about two hours. It was amazing. The view of Florida was breath-taking, and we got to see the sunrise. Deep down I think Mum and Dad were nervous. They tried to hide it but I just knew!

We flew over the tourist attractions and made our way

over swampland. The pilot lowered our craft to the treetops and skimmed through the upper branches. In the next cleared areas, we lowered the baskets to about ten feet off the ground in search of crocodiles, unfortunately without success. We discovered some wildlife in the shape of wild turkeys. We followed them at a safe distance. I don't know who was more excited, them or us! We then made our way to the landing site. This was on a local golf site. The pilot advised the final touch down would be a crash landing but not to worry. We came down safe and sound and we all helped to pack up the equipment. We were then given certificates and champagne to celebrate a successful trip. This ended our first week which was in Orlando. This experience was definitely a nine out of ten for me, a lifetime experience!

My next adventure was a holiday in Tunisia arranged by Scope. I travelled with my friend Heulwen, making a total of thirteen members, headed by the group leader Mike. My other friends from Scope, who were also in wheelchairs, were there. The first couple of days were spent sightseeing and relaxing on the beach. The weather was hot and humid but the sea gave us an opportunity to cool down. A lot of water sports were taking place. We all tried the banana ride. The boat looks like a large giant banana. There were four of us in our banana boat. You all sit behind each other. I was at the back being held by Heulwen. We were pulled really fast through the water. We didn't fall off. I kept my eyes closed the whole time!

One day, Mike, the organiser of the holiday, said, "Anyone fancy a go at paragliding tomorrow morning?"

Five of us said yes but we thought it was a joke. Little did we know.

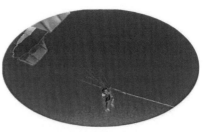

Bang! Bang! on the door the next morning.

There stood Mike ready for paragliding.

It wasn't a joke!

"Good morning! Ready for it today?"

Excited, shocked and nervous I really thought it was a joke but I thought I'm ready for this.

I was third to go up. You can do this I was thinking. It was wonderful. I felt happy, excited, exhilarated. I wasn't at all nervous. The experience was wonderful. Mike was the last to go up. We could all see how nervous he was, but he had to go. I think he was scared. We were all laughing at him. We all had a good laugh with him when he came down!

Me and Heulwen called Mum and Dad that night on the phone telling them all about our day. They found it hard to take it in.

Mum said, "Is everyone OK? Is Alicia OK?"

Heulwen said, "Of course Brenda, nine out of ten experience!"

On a day trip to Derbyshire with Scope, we were all invited to visit the local hang-gliding event. After my experience paragliding in Tunisia, I had always wanted to give it a go. The team leader was a professional lady who was very experienced. She asked me if I would like to try ensuring me it would be perfectly safe. I was attached to her back with a safety harness and away we went. Hang gliding is something I'd always wanted to do. I'd been waiting for a long time to do this. I felt happy, excited, exhilarated, fearless, even calm…Someone went up with me. They talked me through what to expect. I wasn't at all nervous. But it wasn't what I expected. I was surprised by how high I went. And there was no sound. It was very quiet. I could see the tops of trees and all the fields. It was very cold, especially on my head. I could feel the air when it rushed over the top of my head. I really enjoyed it and I was sad when it was all over! Little did we know a passing motorist had stopped in a layby and was watching what was going on. He couldn't believe his eyes seeing me being taken out of my wheelchair and sailing through the air. Photographs were taken and sent to us with an accompanying letter.

17 Portland Terrace
Langwith
Mansfield
Notts NG209HA


Dear Friends,

I was at Darby Dale Airway on Thursday last (17.9) with my own family party and captured a few photos of some of your group in the act of flying. One of the staff gave me your address to send some prints.

I hope you like the results. They may not be as sharp as I would like but – you were moving!

My family and I were very impressed at how brave you all were – Well done.

I haven't got your names other than Mike Flood who may be the Brave Flyer# 1. Braveiarter # 2 was the young man who followed him, and 'Freeflyer' #3 was a young lady who uses a wheelchair when on the ground – bet it was good to be out of your chariot for a short while.

Me, I'm a chicken without wings! I stayed on the ground and sent 82-year-old Granny and 79-year-old Grandad up instead!

Keep having your adventure guys and gals. Follow your dreams!

Yours truly,

Dave Crump, retired social worker former carer of a dear friend who is physically/mentally unable to do as you young people have done (and can now prove it!!!)


While in the air, I forgot I had a disability. It was amazing. Hang gliding gets nine out of ten! Live life to the full.

# Chapter Nine
## Where I Am Now

With very little opportunity for volunteer work, keeping active is a must. For the past five years, I have been a member of the Chester Sports Club for people with disabilities. We meet on a Saturday from twelve till three. The club is run by volunteers. Both Mum and Dad help to run the club, which has 50 members. We take part in many indoor sports, ranging from badminton, handball, carpet bowls and indoor cricket. The session starts with warm-up relay races and ball games. This is usually followed by handball. After a short break, the second session takes place with badminton and more ball games in the sports hall. Every week in the gym, carpet bowls, yoga and Zumba take place. On alternate Saturdays, all forms of disabilities are catered for at the club, varying from autism, cerebral palsy, downs syndrome to people with learning difficulties.

The yoga session has given me another valuable leisure activity. Claudia the lady who volunteers to give yoga therapy at the club is also a professional therapist. I have a half session each Monday with her, giving me much-needed use of my limbs which I can't use due to my disability. Yoga is good for my body and mind. I enjoy the movements and relaxation. My yoga teacher plays very soothing music at the end of each session. I feel that my body is more loose, so I am in more control of my arms and legs. At the moment I go once a week but I'm hoping to increase the sessions. I would recommend yoga to people in wheelchairs.

Many years ago, the lads at our local club raised some money to buy me a three-wheeler bike. Unfortunately, I outgrew it after a couple of years and was unable to find a suitable replacement. I recently donated the bike to my old school.

Recently, I went with my carer and friend Katie to do some bike riding at New Scene Chester. Katie was pedalling at the front, me at the back. I was very surprised at myself on a bike after almost twenty years of not cycling. I can't believe how successful I was! I'm excited about this bike ride. I'm definitely going to do more of it in the near future.

My support worker Sue also advised of a cycling club at Alyn Waters near Wrexham. We try to go most Fridays depending on the weather. When we are there, we can hire several different adapted bicycles. Two-seater bikes with three wheels, electric bikes and tandems are available to hire. The electric bike is our favourite, as we can speed around the park and go fast down the hills. The fresh breeze hitting your face is lovely and the views are beautiful.

I have started wheelchair ice skating at Deeside Ice rink. I go once a month. You can't keep up with me I go so fast! Jack, one of the volunteers, holds on to the back of my wheelchair and away we go!

Once a week I go bowling in Wrexham. After the bowling, the group goes out for a meal. I've recently been asked to join the Wolf Bowling Team. I said yes, I would like to be a member of the team so now I'm part of the Wolf Bowling Team!

Last but not least in my sporting activities is swimming. I need help in the water at all times and have to use an inflatable rubber ring. We go as often as we can, both at home and on holiday. Being in the water gives me a great sense of freedom, along with all the exercise benefits.

It may seem all my new hobbies are exercise or sports-related but I do also attend a fortnightly group who discuss disabled people's rights. I really enjoy receiving all the new information and hearing about new opportunities.

Our first activity in Chester Sports Club following the summer break is to take part in a sponsored walk, arranged by the Chester Business Club, where much-needed funds are raised for our club and other local charities. We have a  sponsored walk every year. Where do we start? We start at the racecourse in Chester and halfway through we arrive at the Duke of Westminster's estate. We walk through the estate. We then stop off at Eccleston and some walk along the River Dee. Wheelchair users go back along the road. Dogs have been allowed to go since 2013, so Lottie comes with us. There are about 200 people walking. We raise a lot of money for the sports club.

Our club has been a great benefit to me and I have made some really good friends. The only disappointment is that I can't join in with the lad's Wednesday 7-a-side football!

My friend Pauline was having a chat with my Mum one day about something called Pick 'n' Mix. Pauline gave my Mum a leaflet which told you all about it. I was very interested to see for myself and decided to go along. It was a Monday evening in March 2018. After that first visit, I said to my Mum and Dad, "I'd like to keep coming."

But it was a Bank Holiday Monday the following week so I had to stay home!

Pick 'n' mix is a meeting up for Christian activity.

About halfway through the evening, we have a circle time altogether. It starts with a sensory cushion, which we throw to different people in the circle. When they catch it, it's their turn to share some news about their day. Then they throw it to someone else, and so on…We also have a time of reflection when we consider something that's happened, or pass around an object, or do a role play based on a Bible story. David, one of the people who comes, mans the sound desk. He uses music and sound effects to create a soundscape. One story we sometimes do is about the time Jesus and the disciples went on Lake Galilee in a boat. We use a big parachute to represent the movement of the waves, gentle at first so we have nice calm music. Then it begins to rain and we have a rain sound effect. Then it gets really windy! We make the chute fly over our heads. Then we get a massive clap of thunder. We usually all laugh. The chute goes crazy. Then the disciples wake Jesus, somebody in the circle, and he stands up, holds out his hand and says, "Stop!" Immediately, the sound effects stop and all is calm. This is what I think the story is about: sometimes in our lives, we need to reflect on what's happening; think things out.

I've also thought about how different people come from different beliefs, so we shouldn't be judgemental.

At Christmas, we did a play called *Starry Night*. It was a Nativity play but it wasn't just for children. In fact, lots of different age groups took part. I was a star. Of course! It was my role to open the play and set the scene. The play began with a beautiful piece of music. After a couple of minutes, I came into the performance space and danced like a star! I called up all the other stars to join me, which included one of my friends from Pick 'n' mix – he wafted some starry fabric to the music – and then all the little children from the toddler group, who came running on dressed in silver like me with little starry ribbon sticks. I came on at the end too, after the birth of Jesus. I was very happy and glad to be part of it all. I got lots of lovely comments at the end from the people who came to see it.

I like doing drama. I hope I can be in more plays. I think more drama would be a good idea for Pick 'n' mix. And we should have hand-outs too to give out so that more people can come along.

The reason I like Pick 'n' mix is that it is a very friendly group; lots of different kinds of people to meet and spend time with from all walks of life. There are various things to do in Pick 'n' mix, such as arts and crafts, singing and role play. Pick 'n' mix gives me a chance to think for myself without anybody supporting me. Did I tell you I stay on my own? My Mum and Dad bring me to the church in Flint where Pick 'n' mix happens but then they take Lottie, my dog, for a walk and go to MacDonald's for a coffee. They don't come back for me until it's finished. We mainly play ball games, do colouring and crafts and there are lots of table-top activities, but I like to write. And talk. Using my eye gaze. People are interested in finding out about my eye gaze and how I use it to communicate. When I'm at Pick 'n' mix I like to take the opportunity to talk about my life, my views on things, what I've been up to, and my plans for the future. We have coffee time, altogether usually. It's nice when everyone just chills and chats and even sings with Eldon's guitar.

In 2018, I had one of my mouth and foot pictures printed as Christmas cards. It was good. Mum had some of her pictures printed as Christmas cards too!

A friend got in touch with the Mouth and Foot Association to see if I could join them. The society straight away got in touch with us. They sent me a letter.

**Dear Ms Gough,**
**Please find enclosed information about our association**
**and how to join requested by your friend.**
**Best regards.**
**Bhavni**

And with the letter were all sorts of interesting leaflets about their work. Their leaflet *The Mouth and Foot Painting Artists* shows a selection of lovely paintings by mouth and foot artists. It says:

**The members are professional artists who have no use of their hands because of disability at birth, an accident or through illness, but have learnt to paint by holding a brush in their mouth or between their toes.**

**They decline any charity and are proud to be earning their own living.**

Dad then rang up the Mouth and Foot Association. The society was very helpful. Dad was advised to get in touch with the Mouth and Foot artist Tom Yendell, which he did. Because there's no Mouth and Foot centre near to where we live, Tom Yendell suggested we contact a local art school for general tuition but to practise at home to get used to foot painting again. He said to call any time for help and advice. The Foot and Mouth society have been very supportive.

Recently, I have joined a group in Wrexham which runs pottery classes. We meet in the drama workshops. The class is good. It lets you express your own ideas. You have to find the pot you like and then work on it yourself. Then the teacher glazes it for you. I made a model of an owl. It has been much admired.

Last Summer, I joined an Arts and Craft centre in Wrexham. It's good fun meeting up with such a friendly group. I've made some great things. We do this activity called book art. What happens is you take old books. The books we have used, people don't want any more, and they have donated them to the group. You fold the pages into different shapes. You then remove the cover and book spine. It's sort of like origami We looked at a book about book art, which showed all the different things you could make. I'd like to buy that book. When I'm next in town, I'll have to see if I can find that book and buy it. Using this book art, I've made a birdhouse and three hedgehogs! Well, what happened with the hedgehogs was that my Uncle David, who sometimes visits us on a Sunday, called one Sunday, and when he saw the book art hedgehog he said, "Oh, just look at that hedgehog. It's wonderful!"

So Mum and I decided we'd make one for him and give it to him on his birthday which is on St David's Day. Mum painted on the hedgehog the red Welsh dragon and on St David's Day we gave Uncle David the hedgehog. He was so touched and pleased he cried when we gave it to him.

I also like the Art and Craft centre because at lunchtime we play bingo. If you win you get a bag of sweets. I've won four times!

However, the best of all about the Arts and Craft centre was going to a disco that I was told about at one of the sessions. At the disco, I met up with some of the old friends I used to work with all those years ago. One of these friends, Chris said to me, "I remember you from the S.W.S. group. It's started back up again. Would you like to come to a meeting tomorrow? We'd like to discuss something with you."

How quick was that! I am really looking forward to joining the group and working with them again. I'm so excited about that.

I want to carry on writing. I have started my next book which will be a book of short stories.

I've already written one story, *The Haunted House*!

I will of course continue writing my poems. I want to take part in poetry competitions. For me, writing poems is part of my life. I live my life to make poems. For me, writing poems is just an everyday thing.

With my carer, Katie, I wrote another poem about my Mum.

## For My Mum

I know I don't always say every day
How special you are to me in every way.
You look after me in every way.
Through the laughter and tears,
The stress and the fears,
I hold you so dear.
I speak very little.
You know what I mean.
My thoughts become yours.
You know what I need.
Nothing seems to worry you.
In all you do your strength comes
through.

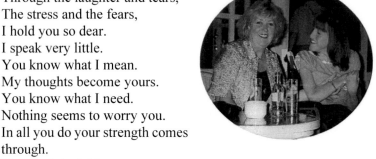

The clock is ticking.
No time for a nap.
You're busy doing ironing and that.
The daily walk of our family dog,
It's your turn, Mum!
The night draws in and we've all been fed.
It's nearly time for our beds.
Your work's not done.
We do a quiz.
You're tired and sleepy but "It's OK hun!"
I always win, never lose.
Night, night, Mum. I love you, Alicia.


I've got so many new ideas and adventures to look forward to and achieve in the future. First being getting this book published and hopefully more books in the future. Then who knows. I am also looking forward to taking up my volunteering job again. And I want to continue to be happy and healthy.

This is the first thirty-five years of my life. I wonder what the next thirty will hold! I wonder if I will achieve my new ideas and adventures. Will I achieve more? Will there be another book? Who knows…

## My Book Poem

I've always liked reading books
But I never thought I would be
the writer.
It has always been a dream of
mine,
Memories floating back to my
mind.

Other people are quite amazed
by my book,
About my memory.
They ask me, "How do you
remember?"
I say to them, "How could I
forget?"
I'm the person who has done it
all!